BTEC FIRST

Health & Social Care

Student Workbook

Mark Walsh and Richard Chaloner

Published by Collins Education
An imprint of HarperCollins Publishers
77–85 Fulham Palace Road
Hammersmith
London
W6 8JB

Browse the complete Collins Education catalogue at
www.collinseducation.com

© HarperCollins Publishers Limited 2010
10 9 8 7 6 5 4 3 2 1

ISBN 978 0 00 734266 2

Mark Walsh and Richard Chaloner assert the moral right to be identified as
the authors of this work.

British Library Cataloguing in Publication Data.
A Catalogue record for this publication is available from the British Library.

Commissioned by Emma Woolf
Edited by Mitch Fitton
Design and typesetting by Thomson Digital
Cover design by Angela English
Picture research by Geoff Holdsworth/Pictureresearch.co.uk
Printed by Martins the Printers

Photographic acknowledgements

Photos.com (2); iStockphoto (5/Loretta Hostettler); Rex Features (8/Andy
Lauwers); iStockphoto (9/Aldo Murillo); iStockphoto (13/Dean Mitchell);
Rex Features (27/Jussi Nukari); iStockphoto (35/syagci); Alamy (36/Stock
Connection Blue).

Contents

1 Communication in health and social care 1

  1.1 Different forms of communication 2

  1.2 Barriers to effective communication 5

2 Individual rights in health and social care 9

  2.1 Diversity and equality in society 10

  2.2 Principles and values in health and social care 13

3 Individual needs in health and social care 17

  3.1 Everyday needs of individuals in society 18

  3.2 Factors influencing the health and needs of individuals 21

  3.3 Planning to meet the health and wellbeing needs of an individual 24

4 Ensuring safe environments in health and social care 27

  4.1 Hazards and risks 28

  4.2 Health and safety legislation 30

  4.3 Risk assessment processes 32

6 Cultural diversity in health and social care 35

  6.1 The diversity of individuals and different religious beliefs and practices 36

  6.2 Beliefs and practices of different religious or secular groups 37

  6.3 Factors that influence equality of opportunity 38

  6.4 Legislation, codes of practice and charters 40

Glossary 43

Student notes 45

Introduction

This workbook is made up of questions and activities that cover each section of Units 1, 2, 3, 4 and 6 of the BTEC First in Health and Social Care qualification. The questions and activities are designed to develop and assess your knowledge and understanding of a range of topics that are part of these units. To get the most out of using this workbook as part of your BTEC First in Health and Social Care studies, you need to understand that:

▶ What you learn from studying Units 1, 2, 3, 4 and 6 with your class tutors, and from using a textbook written for the BTEC First Health and Social Care qualification, will provide you with the background knowledge needed to complete the questions and activities in this workbook.

▶ You should complete the questions and activities after you have studied the corresponding part of each unit using textbooks and other resources with your tutor or as your tutor directs.

▶ It is best to complete the questions and activities for each unit before you begin any of the assessment tasks associated with each unit. Completing the questions and activities to the best of your ability will help to prepare you for these important assessments.

▶ The mark allocations and the number of answer lines provided for each question or activity are a guide to how much you should write.

▶ Where a question asks you to provide a specific number of examples ('Give three examples of...') or to identify a specific number of reasons ('Describe two reasons why...'), your answer must provide the specified number of items to achieve full marks. Providing more examples or more reasons than the question requires will not gain you any more marks, so it is best not to do this.

When Edexcel set controlled assessment tasks and assignment questions they choose their words very carefully. You need to understand that the way a question is asked or the way a task is worded is very important. Always make sure that you look at, understand and respond to the command verb – for example, 'describe', 'explain' – in order to get the right level of detail in your answer. 'Name' and 'give' are low-level question verbs for 1 or 2 marks; 'describe' usually requires more detail for 2 or more marks; 'explain' typically requires more detail again, and 'evaluate' requires the most detail.

Finally, when answering questions, make sure that you write clearly and spell correctly. This is very important when using the specialist words and phrases of the health and social care field.

Answers can be found at: www.collinseducation.com/btechsc

Communication in health and social care

This unit covers the following topics:

▶ ways of promoting effective communication in care settings

▶ barriers to effective communication.

Your learning in this unit will be assessed through assignments that are set and marked by your tutor in accordance with grading criteria and standards set by Edexcel. The assignments will require you to focus on:

▶ different forms and methods of communication

▶ factors which ensure that communication is effective

▶ the range of barriers that can prevent effective communication from occurring and ways of overcoming these barriers.

The questions and activities that follow provide you with an opportunity to develop your knowledge and assess your understanding of the range of topics that are part of Unit 1.

Answers can be found at: www.collinseducation.com/btechsc

1.1 Different forms of communication

A person working in a health or social care setting may communicate every day with a variety of other people, including colleagues, workers from other organisations, people who use services (clients) and their relatives and friends. As a result, care practitioners need to understand and use a range of different forms of communication. The questions and activities that follow provide you with opportunities to develop and show your understanding of:

▶ *contexts of communication:* e.g. one-to-one; groups; informal; with colleagues, managers, people using services

▶ *different forms of communication:* e.g. verbal and non-verbal; body language; facial expression; touch or contact; use of signs, symbols, pictures, objects of reference; writing; technological aids

▶ *alternative forms of communication:* e.g. use of sign language, lip reading, Makaton, signs and symbols, Braille, technological aids; human aids (e.g. interpreters, translators, signers).

Questions and activities

Chloe has received a letter inviting her to an interview at Rivermead Nursery next week. The letter from Debbie Meadows, the nursery manager, says that the interview will focus on Chloe's reasons for wanting to work with children and will be an opportunity for her to demonstrate her communication skills. Chloe is excited about visiting the nursery but a little worried about having her communication skills assessed. Chloe's tutor has reassured her that she just needs to put into practice the things she has learnt about in class.

1. After introducing herself and checking that Chloe was comfortable and ready to start her interview, Debbie Meadows' first question was, 'Can you identify two different forms of communication that might be used by nursery workers when they interact with the children or their parents at Rivermead Nursery?' If you were in Chloe's position, what would you say? **(2 marks)**

_____

_____

_____

_____

2. Chloe was next asked to describe three reasons why nursery workers need to develop and use effective communication skills at work. What three reasons would you give? **(3 marks)**

Reason 1 _____

_____

Reason 2 _____

_____

Reason 3 _____

_____

3. Chloe's teacher advised her that she should have a good understanding of non-verbal communication, as this is important when working in care settings. Using your own words, explain what the term 'non-verbal communication' means. **(3 marks)**

_____

_____

_____

_____

4. Describe three ways in which a child at a nursery might express their feelings through non-verbal communication methods. **(3 marks)**

_____

_____

_____

_____

_____

_____

Gina has recently started work as a support worker at Serafina House residential home. During her induction programme she works alongside Pauline, an experienced registered nurse. Gina has spent the morning meeting a new resident, Mrs Marshall, who is anxious about moving into the home. Pauline has asked Gina to spend some time with Mrs Marshall so that she feels supported and more comfortable in her new surroundings. As she left to go a meeting, Pauline said, 'Remember Gina, it's all about using your communication skills.'

5. Explain how Gina could use her verbal and non-verbal communication skills to reassure Mrs Marshall and make her feel more comfortable and included in the activities of Serafina House. **(6 marks)**

_____

_____

_____

_____

_____

_____

_____

_____

Pauline meets with Gina every month to discuss her progress and to try to help Gina with any problems or issues that are affecting her at work. During a recent supervision session, Gina asked Pauline what 'active listening' involved because Philip, one of the deputy home managers, said everyone had to try and improve their 'active listening' skills.

6. Explain what 'active listening' involves, and give two examples of ways that Gina could demonstrate active listening when she communicates with Mrs Marshall. **(7 marks)**

_____

_____

_____

_____

_____

_____

_____

7. Describe how Gina could use touch and physical contact appropriately when she communicates with Mrs Marshall or other residents at the home. **(4 marks)**

_____

_____

_____

_____

_____

_____

Philip has invited Gina and Pauline to attend a meeting with Mrs Marshall and her son to discuss how Mrs Marshall feels about the care she is receiving at Serafina House. Because this is a formal meeting, Philip has written an agenda and is responsible for chairing and making notes about what people say.

8. Describe three differences between formal and informal communication. **(3 marks)**

_____

_____

_____

_____

_____

_____

9. Give two reasons why it is important that a formal meeting, like the one Philip has organised, has a person 'chairing' or leading the meeting. **(2 marks)**

Reason 1 _____

Reason 2 _____

10. Explain how people at a meeting (like the one Philip has organised) use the communication cycle to interact with each other in an effective way. **(12 marks)**

_____

_____

_____

_____

_____

_____

_____

_____

_____

_____

_____

_____

_____

_____

_____

1.2 Barriers to effective communication

Several factors influence an individual's ability to communicate effectively. These factors are sometimes also referred to as 'barriers' to communication. Knowing and understanding about these different factors or barriers can help a care practitioner to modify the way they communicate with others to ensure that their communication is effective. The questions and activities that follow provide you with opportunities to develop and show your understanding of:

▶ _the communication cycle_: ideas occur; message coded; message sent; message received; message decoded; message understood

▶ _factors that affect communication_: e.g. sensory deprivation; foreign language; jargon; slang; dialect; use of acronyms; cultural differences; distress; emotional difficulties; disability; health issues; environmental problems; misinterpretation of message; differing humour; inappropriate behaviour; aggression; assertiveness

▶ _ways of overcoming communication barriers_: e.g. adapting the environment; understanding language needs and preferences; using the individual's preferred language; timing; electronic devices (text phones, telephone amplifiers, hearing loops).

Questions and activities

Nasrine Chouaki, aged 25, came to the United Kingdom to live with her husband Zaid a year ago. Zaid has lived in the UK for 2 years and works as a restaurant manager. Nasrine is now 3 months' pregnant and wants to find out about prenatal and maternity services in her local area.

However, Nasrine is finding it difficult to obtain the kinds of information she needs. Nasrine has a hearing impairment and cannot understand spoken or written English very well. She is able to lip-read when someone speaks in Arabic and can also read and write fluently in Arabic.

1. Identify two reasons why communication with staff working in local prenatal and maternity services could be difficult for Nasrine. **(2 marks)**

   Reason 1 _____

   Reason 2 _____

2. Describe two things that care practitioners working in local prenatal and maternity services could do to help Nasrine overcome the language barriers that she is facing when trying to obtain care. **(4 marks)**

   _____
   _____
   _____
   _____

3. Explain what the term 'cultural differences' refers to and describe how they might affect care workers' ability to communicate effectively with Nasrine. **(6 marks)**

   _____
   _____
   _____
   _____
   _____
   _____
   _____
   _____

4. Produce a list of five guidance points that could be given to care workers to enable them to understand and communicate more effectively with people, like Nasrine, who have hearing impairments. **(5 marks)**

   Point 1 _____

   Point 2 _____

   Point 3 _____

   Point 4 _____

   Point 5 _____

Edgar Jones is 66 years of age. He has recently had a stroke and is currently receiving care in a specialist stroke ward at his local hospital. The stroke has affected Edgar's ability to speak. He can understand what his wife Doreen says to him but seems unable to respond clearly. Edgar also looks confused and frustrated when some of the doctors speak to him about his 'CVA', his 'meds' and his 'hemiplegia'. One of the nurses explained to Doreen that these terms are medical jargon for a stroke (CVA = cerebrovascular accident), medication and the weakness he has down the right side of his body.

5. Identify two communication barriers that Edgar faces. **(2 marks)**

_____

_____

6. Explain why Edgar seems to be having difficulty communicating with the doctors who come to speak with him. **(2 marks)**

_____

_____

7. Investigate the causes of a 'stroke' (cerebrovascular accident) and the impact it can have on an individual like Edgar. Summarise your findings under the headings: Causes; Physical effects; Effect on communication skills. **(15 marks)**

_____

_____

_____

_____

_____

_____

_____

_____

_____

_____

_____

_____

_____

_____

_____

_____

_____

People who use care services can experience communication problems because of disability, illness or because they are unable to understand the English language. Advocates, interpreters and technological aids can be used to overcome some of the communication barriers that people face.

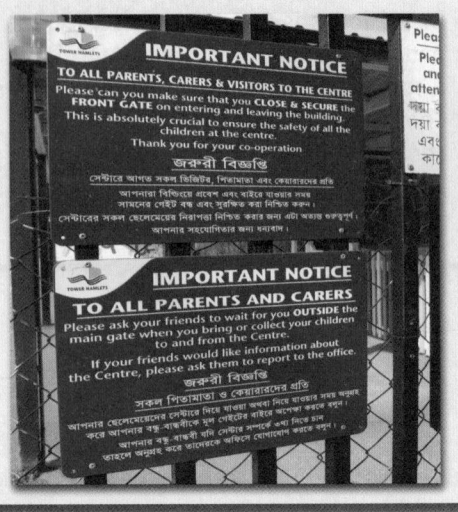

8. Using your own words, explain what an 'advocate' is. Give an example of a care-related situation where an advocate may be used to promote effective communication. **(6 marks)**

_____

_____

_____

_____

_____

_____

_____

_____

9. Identify three examples of electronic devices that can be used to help people to overcome some of the communication barriers that they face as a result of hearing or visual impairment. **(3 marks)**

_____

_____

_____

_____

_____

10. What is an interpreter? Using your own words, explain what an interpreter does. Describe an example of a care situation where an interpreter might be needed to promote effective communication. **(4 marks)**

_____

_____

_____

_____

Individual rights in health and social care

This unit covers the following topics:

▶ diversity and equality in society

▶ principles and values used in care.

Your learning in this unit will be assessed through assignments that are set and marked by your tutor in accordance with grading criteria and standards set by Edexcel. The assignments will require you to focus on:

▶ diversity and equality issues affecting people in the UK

▶ care values and principles and the ways they can be used to promote the rights of people who use services and their relatives.

The questions and activities that follow provide you with an opportunity to develop your knowledge and assess your understanding of the range of topics that are part of Unit 2.

Answers can be found at: www.collinseducation.com/btechsc

2.1 Diversity and equality in society

The UK is a multicultural and socially diverse society. This means that the population consists of a range of ethnic groups who speak a number of languages, hold diverse beliefs and have differing cultural backgrounds. The social and cultural diversity of the population presents care practitioners and care organisations with a challenge – to ensure that the needs and rights of everyone who uses the services are met while also respecting cultural differences. The questions and activities that follow provide you with opportunities to develop and show your understanding of:

▶ *social factors that affect diversity*: e.g. culture, ethnicity, gender, sexuality, age, family structure, social class, geographical location

▶ *political factors that promote equality*: e.g. role of legislation; role of policy, welfare state, delivery of health and social care services

▶ *equality*: e.g. non-discriminatory practice; discriminatory practice (e.g. stereotyping, labelling, prejudice)

▶ *biological factors*: physical features; disabilities (e.g. learning; physical).

Questions and activities

Samira has just started her first day in her new job as a healthcare assistant at the Pinebridge Health Centre. It is her first post since finishing her college course, and Samira is shadowing the practice nurse, Sandra Williams. Sandra is helping Samira to become familiar with the work of the health centre and the people it serves. The Pinebridge Health Centre is in a built-up area that Samira does not know too well, just outside the city centre. Samira wants to find out more about the local population and their needs. She knows that this an important first step in carrying out her new job successfully.

1. Sandra tells Samira that the Pinebridge Health Centre serves a very diverse local community. Describe what you think Sandra meant when she said that the local community was 'diverse'? **(2 marks)**

_____

_____

_____

_____

2. There are several different faith groups in the local area, and the Health Centre caters for people with a range of religious beliefs. Sandra says that this is one of the ways in which the community is diverse. Identify three other forms of diversity. **(3 marks)**

_____

_____

_____

_____

_____

_____

3. Samira finds out that people from a range of cultural backgrounds use the services of Pinebridge Health Centre. Describe three ways in which culture can have an effect on a person's way of life. **(3 marks)**

Effect 1 _____

_____

Effect 2 _____

_____

Effect 3 _____

_____

The Pinebridge Health Centre has equal opportunities policies to help maintain the standard of their service. Sandra explains that these policies help the staff to provide a good quality of care for all their clients. She tells Samira that these policies help the health centre to meet the requirements of equal opportunities legislation.

4. Sandra tells Samira that it is important to understand and respect the diversity in the local community. She says that they must avoid stereotyping people. Describe what is meant by the term 'stereotyping', and explain why the health centre staff must avoid stereotyping their clients. **(6 marks)**

_____

_____

_____

_____

_____

_____

_____

_____

_____

5. In your own words describe what is meant by the term 'equal opportunities legislation'. **(2 marks)**

_____

_____

6. Explain how the health centre's equal opportunities policies can help the centre to provide good quality care for all clients. **(6 marks)**

_____

_____

_____

_____

_____

_____

_____

_____

Rhaman Siddiqui is 78 years old and lives in the Pinebridge area. Rhaman and his wife live in a large house, together with their daughter, their son, and his wife and children. Jenny Williams is a 23-year-old single parent who lives with her 8-month-old son in a small flat across the road from the Siddiqui family.

7. Rhaman and Jenny live in households with different family structures. Identify the type of family that they each belong to. **(2 marks)**

   Rhaman _____

   Jenny _____

8. What is the name of the Act of Parliament that protects Jenny from discrimination on the basis of her gender? **(2 marks)**

   _____

   _____

The Siddiqui family are Muslims. Rahman came to live in the UK from India 40 years ago, and has a good pension from his successful career as an accountant. His son works as a solicitor. Jenny gave up her part-time job when she became pregnant and is dependent on benefits. She is a vegetarian and has no religious faith. Rhaman and Jenny attend clinics at the Pinebridge Health Centre. Rhaman attends a chiropody clinic, and Jenny comes to the mother and baby clinic.

9. Sandra says that Rhaman and Jenny are examples of how the health centre caters for diversity. Apart from family structure, can you describe four ways in which Rhaman and Jenny are different from each other? **(8 marks)**

   Difference 1 _____

   _____

   Difference 2 _____

   _____

   Difference 3 _____

   _____

   Difference 4 _____

   _____

10. Explain how equal opportunities legislation can help people like Rhaman and Jenny to be treated equally and fairly. **(6 marks)**

   _____

   _____

   _____

   _____

   _____

   _____

   _____

   _____

2.2 Principles and values in health and social care

Care principles and values are an important part of care practice. All care workers should know about and use principles and values when they relate to and interact with people who use care services. Care practitioners often use values and principles to promote equality and challenge discriminatory practice. As a result, using principles and values in practice provides a care practitioner with an important way of promoting the rights of people who use services and their families. The questions and activities that follow provide you with opportunities to develop and show your understanding of:

▶ *ethical considerations*: e.g. right-to-life; social justice; person-centred approach; the expectations of individuals receiving the service; empathy; honesty; adherence to codes of practice and policies

▶ *individual rights*: e.g. rights to be respected; treated equally and not discriminated against; treated as an individual; treated in a dignified way; allowed privacy; safeguarded from danger and harm; allowed access to information about themselves; able to communicate using their preferred methods of communication and language; supported in a way that meets their needs; takes account of their choices and protects them

▶ *worker responsibilities*: e.g. provision of active support to enable people who use services to communicate their needs, views and preferences; use of communication to support diversity, inclusion and promote equality of opportunity; confidentiality; disclosure; dealing with tensions between rights and responsibilities; importance of accurate recording; storage and retrieving information of information (including electronic methods); filing correctly and securely; the requirements of the Data Protection Act 1998 and the Freedom of Information Act 2005.

Questions and activities

Jasmine is a health and social care student, and is carrying out her work placement as a care assistant at The Lodge Care Home. The Lodge provides residential care for older people, and has 30 residents. Most of the residents need some support to dress, wash and use the toilet. The Lodge has a commitment to supporting individual rights, and Jasmine has been told to look at The Lodges' policies and code of practice. She will need to put them into practice when working with the residents.

1. The care home manager, Diane, tells Jasmine that the policies and code of practice at The Lodge are based on care principles and values. She asks Jasmine if she can explain what care principles and values are. What would you answer? **(3 marks)**

_____

_____

_____

_____

2. One of the care values that The Lodge upholds is to show respect towards the residents, and support their right to dignity and privacy. Explain how Jasmine could put this into practice when she is working with residents. **(6 marks)**

_____

_____

_____

_____

_____

_____

_____

_____

3. The Lodge has a policy of giving the residents choice, and allowing them to make their own decisions. Identify two reasons why it is important to give residents choice. **(4 marks)**

Reason 1 _____

_____

Reason 2 _____

_____

4. Explain what the term 'empowerment' means. **(2 marks)**

_____

_____

Alice is 79 years of age and lives on her own in a small bungalow. She suffers from osteoarthritis and is unable to carry out household tasks unaided. Alice is also hearing impaired, and uses lip reading to help her communicate. Since she was diagnosed with arthritis Alice has taken a positive attitude. She has tried to carry on doing things for herself whenever possible and likes to prepare her own food.

Alice receives daily visits from a home care worker. Alice's usual carer has moved to another job and a new carer, Sarah, has been visiting her for the past few days. Sarah works very quickly and carries out all the household tasks while listening to her music player with mini headphones. She also prepares food that she thinks will be suitable for Alice. Sarah lets herself in with her key, whereas the previous carer used to knock and wait for Alice to answer the door. Alice is beginning to feel unhappy about the care she is receiving.

5. Identify two care principles or values that Sarah is failing to put into practice when she is working with Alice. **(2 marks)**

Value 1 _____

Value 2 _____

6. Explain how Sarah could change the way she works so that she is supporting Alice's right to be able to communicate effectively. **(6 marks)**

_____

_____

_____

_____

_____

_____

_____

_____

7. Explain three reasons why care principles and values are important when providing support for people like Alice. **(6 marks)**

Reason 1 _____

_____

Reason 2 _____

_____

Reason 3 _____

_____

Anne is one of the youth workers at the First Stop Drop-in Centre. The centre is based in an inner city housing estate, and offers help and support to young people. Many local teenagers come to the centre. Kellie is 15 years old and lives with her mother in a small flat on the estate. She visits the centre and asks Anne for a private chat. Kellie asks Anne if she will keep what she tells her secret, and Anne agrees. Kellie then says that her best friend, Amy (also 15 years of age), is being abused by Amy's stepfather. Amy has told Kellie she is angry, upset and frightened by what her stepfather has done but doesn't want anyone else to know. Anne is shocked and tells Kellie that she will have to report what is happening. Kellie becomes angry and says that she thought her information would remain confidential.

8. Explain why Anne felt that she couldn't keep the situation that Kellie has told her about a secret. **(4 marks)**

_____

_____

_____

_____

9. Anne feels that she handled the conversation with Kellie badly. If you were in Anne's position, how would you have dealt with the conversation? **(4 marks)**

_____

_____

_____

_____

10. Care workers have a responsibility to maintain client confidentiality and a responsibility to protect clients from harm. Can you list four other responsibilities that care workers have? **(4 marks)**

Responsibility 1 _____

Responsibility 2 _____

Responsibility 3 _____

Responsibility 4 _____

Individual needs in health and social care

This unit covers the following topics:

▶ the everyday needs of individuals in society

▶ factors that influence the health and needs of individuals

▶ planning to meet the health and wellbeing needs of an individual.

Your learning in this unit will be assessed through assignments that are set and marked by your tutor in accordance with grading criteria and standards set by Edexcel. The assignments will require you to focus on:

▶ the range of needs people of all ages have in order to grow, develop and achieve good health and wellbeing

▶ the different types of factors that influence the health and needs of individuals across the lifespan

▶ creating a health improvement plan for an individual.

The questions and activities that follow provide you with an opportunity to develop your knowledge and assess your understanding of the range of topics that are part of Unit 3.

Answers can be found at: www.collinseducation.com/btechsc

3.1 Everyday needs of individuals in society

People who are in the same age group, or life stage such as infancy, adulthood or old age, have a similar range of basic, everyday needs. These needs are the requirements every individual has in order to:

▶ be physically healthy (physical needs)

▶ develop their knowledge, skills and abilities (intellectual needs)

▶ develop communication skills and personal relationships (social needs)

▶ feel secure and have good mental health (emotional needs).

The questions and activities that follow provide you with opportunities to develop and show your understanding of:

▶ *the importance of needs*: Maslow's hierarchy in relation to physical, intellectual, emotional and social needs

▶ *physical needs*: importance of, for example, food, water, shelter, warmth, exercise, sleep, safety, security

▶ *intellectual needs*: e.g. learning, achievement, mental activity

▶ *emotional needs*: importance of, for example, relationships, affection, love, self-concept, fulfilment, respect

▶ *social needs*: importance of, for example, family, friends, group membership, community; sense of belonging, acceptance

▶ *spiritual needs*: importance of, for example, personal beliefs, religion

▶ *needs in relation to life stages*: infancy, childhood, adulthood, later adulthood.

Questions and activities

Care workers need to understand the types of needs that individuals have. The American psychologist, Abraham Maslow, suggested a way of looking at people's needs. He used a pyramid shape to illustrate his ideas (shown on the right). This way of looking at needs is known as 'Maslow's hierarchy of needs'. Maslow's hierarchy of needs is well known in the field of health and social care.

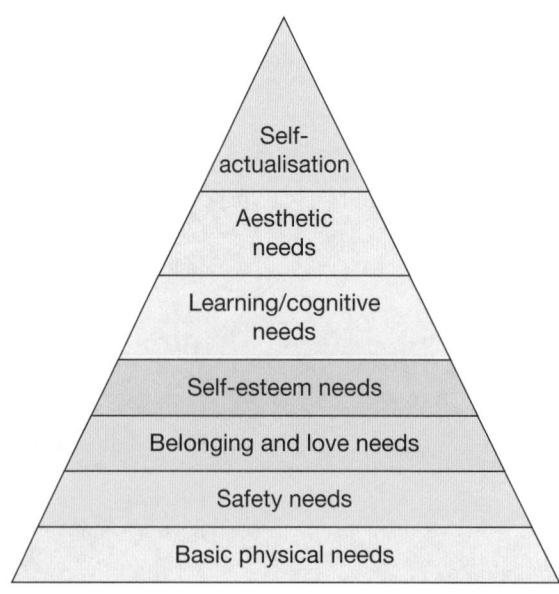

1. Maslow's ideas about needs are referred to as a hierarchy. What do you think the term 'hierarchy' means? **(2 marks)**

   _____

   _____

2. Basic physical needs are shown as the bottom layer in Maslow's pyramid of needs. Can you explain why physical needs are at the bottom of the pyramid? **(3 marks)**

   _____

   _____

   _____

   _____

3. Needs are sometimes put into categories using the letters PIESS. In this classification the first letter, P, stands for physical needs. What do the other letters stand for? **(4 marks)**

   I stands for _____

   E stands for _____

   S stands for _____

   S stands for _____

   Emma is 18 years old and is a single parent. She lives in a one-bedroom flat with her daughter, Sharne, who is 1 year old. Emma gave up her college course when she found that she was pregnant. She now cares for Sharne full time, and finds it hard to make time to meet up with her friends. Emma feels she is losing touch with them. Emma sometimes says that she misses her college course, because she was enjoying learning new things in her studies.

4. As an infant Sharne is dependent on her mother Emma for many of her needs to be met. List three physical needs that Sharne has at her life stage. **(3 marks)**

   Need 1 _____

   Need 2 _____

   Need 3 _____

5. Emma is determined to give her daughter the best possible start in life and to ensure that all her needs are being met. Describe how Emma could support Sharne's emotional needs. **(4 marks)**

   _____

   _____

   _____

   _____

6. Can you describe two areas of need that Emma has that are not being met? Explain how Emma may be affected by this. **(6 marks)**

_____

_____

_____

_____

_____

_____

_____

_____

7. As Sharne grows up she will enter the life stage of childhood. Emma plans to take Sharne to a local playgroup when she is old enough. Describe how attending a playgroup can support a child's intellectual and social needs. **(4 marks)**

_____

_____

_____

_____

_____

_____

George is 82 years old and lives in a small flat in sheltered accommodation. He moved there 2 years ago, after suffering a stroke. Since the stroke George has suffered from mobility problems and is visually impaired. He seldom leaves his flat. George has a care worker, Faye, who calls on him daily. They get on well and chat to each other during her visits. George tells Faye that if it wasn't for her visits he wouldn't see anyone on most days. Faye carries out the household tasks that George cannot do for himself and helps George to wash and dress. She also makes sure that he is eating an adequate and balanced diet. George used to be a PE teacher and was a keen member of an amateur history society. Nowadays he spends most of his time alone listening to the radio and he misses being able to read extensively like he used to.

8. Identify two areas of need that Faye is supporting when she visits George. **(2 marks)**

Need 1 _____

Need 2 _____

9. Explain how George's needs have changed as he had a stroke. **(6 marks)**

_____

_____

_____

_____

_____

_____

_____

_____

10. Identify two areas of need that George has that are not being met adequately at the moment. Explain why you think they are not being met. **(6 marks)**

Area of need 1 _____

_____

_____

Area of need 2 _____

_____

_____

3.2 Factors influencing the health and needs of individuals

An individual's everyday or basic needs change over time as they get older and develop. An individual's particular needs may also change and vary as result of various factors relating to their physical, social and cultural background and their lifestyle. The questions and activities that follow provide you with opportunities to develop and show your understanding of:

▶ _socio-economic factors_: e.g. social class; employment; culture; living conditions; income; education

▶ _physical factors_: e.g. genetic inheritance; disability; sensory impairment; age; gender; environment (e.g. water and sanitation, pollution)

▶ _lifestyle factors_: e.g. personal hygiene; diet; exercise; smoking; substance misuse; stress; working patterns; sexual practices; social and community networks

▶ _health factors_: e.g. infection; injury; mental health; presence of chronic disorder.

Questions and activities

Simon is 28 years old and works in a busy estate agent's office. Simon is keen to get on and works long hours, often missing lunch to get work finished. Sometimes he brings work home. Simon likes to 'work hard and play hard' as he puts it, and in the evenings he often meets friends in the pub. He usually drinks a few pints of his favourite strong lager and eats a takeaway meal on the way home. At weekends he plays football with a local team and likes to drink with friends in the pub afterwards. Simon is a smoker and he gets through about 20 cigarettes a day.

1. Explain the health risks that Simon could face if he continues to smoke cigarettes. **(6 marks)**

_____

_____

_____

_____

_____

_____

_____

_____

2. Simon admits that he should give up smoking. He knows that it is an unhealthy pastime. Identify three other lifestyle factors that could affect Simon's health in a negative way. **(3 marks)**

Factor 1 _____

Factor 2 _____

Factor 3 _____

3. Identify one aspect of Simon's lifestyle that could be having a positive effect on his health and wellbeing, and explain how it could benefit him. **(4 marks)**

_____

_____

_____

_____

_____

4. Simon has recently visited his GP. He says that he has begun to suffer from persistent headaches and that he is not sleeping well. Also he says that his appetite has gone down and he is finding it hard to concentrate at work. Which aspect of Simon's lifestyle is a possible cause of these symptoms? **(2 marks)**

_____

_____

Owen and Nia Lloyd have three children of school age and live in a housing association flat in a crowded inner city area. Owen has been unemployed since the cleaning firm he worked for closed down 18 months ago. Owen left school at 16 with no formal qualifications and has been unable to find another job. Nia works part time on the checkout at a local supermarket. She doesn't like her job, but has to do it as the family find it hard to make ends meet.

The Forster family live in a five-bedroom detached house. Alan Forster works as a solicitor and his wife Rose is a dentist. They both have high levels of job satisfaction. They have one son who is at boarding school. The Forsters enjoy regular holidays abroad and are members of a private health and fitness club.

5. The Lloyd family and the Forster family have different socio-economic factors affecting them. One of the ways they are different is that the Forsters are in a higher social class than the Lloyds. Can you describe three other socio-economic differences between the Lloyds and the Forsters? **(6 marks)**

Difference 1 _____

_____

Difference 2 _____

_____

Difference 3 _____

_____

6. Explain two ways that social class can affect a person's life chances and their health and wellbeing. **(4 marks)**

_____

_____

_____

_____

7. The Forsters have well-paid jobs and a high level of job satisfaction. Explain how this can affect their health and wellbeing. **(4 marks)**

_____

_____

_____

_____

3.3 Planning to meet the health and wellbeing needs of an individual

An individual's health and wellbeing needs may not be met if, for example, they adopt an unhealthy lifestyle and become physically unfit. Health and social care workers can help people to meet their needs by developing individual health improvement plans and supporting them to achieve short-, medium- and long-term health improvement goals. The questions and activities that follow provide you with opportunities to develop and show your understanding of:

▶ *needs*: taking into account as appropriate, for example, physical, social, emotional, intellectual; health needs arising from a desire to improve an individual's health (e.g. losing weight, giving up smoking, reducing alcohol intake)

▶ *assessment of general health and wellbeing*: questioning to obtain information relevant to health and wellbeing (e.g. in an interview, using a questionnaire); physical measurements (e.g. height, weight, pulse rate, respiration on exertion); interpretation (e.g. factors relevant to the individual contributing positively and negatively to health and wellbeing); calculation of BMI; state of health as indicated by physical measurements

▶ *plan*: setting short-term and longer-term targets for improving health; action plan for individual to meet needs and targets; how progress in meeting targets will be monitored.

Questions and activities

Sabhia is a health improvement worker in a community health team. Josh is a client of the team and has asked for advice to improve his health and fitness. Josh is 35 years old and he works in an office. He drinks several pints of beer each day and has not taken regular exercise since leaving school. Josh smokes about 15 cigarettes a day and eats takeaway food several times a week. He has come to the centre because he has been feeling out of breath recently and is worried about his weight. Josh's height is 180 cm and his weight is 104 kg. Sabhia tells him that his BMI is 32 and this means that he is obese and needs to lose weight. Sabhia has drawn up a health improvement plan for Josh to follow. The plan has short-, medium- and long-term targets to help Josh to gradually improve his health.

1. Describe what the term 'BMI' means. Explain how it can be used to assess a person's level of health and fitness. **(4 marks)**

_____

_____

_____

_____

2. One of the targets that Sabhia sets for Josh is to regulate his eating by having a more balanced diet. Can you list three other health improvement targets that could be part of a health improvement plan for Josh? **(3 marks)**

Target 1 _____

Target 2 _____

Target 3 _____

3. Explain why having short-, medium- and long-term targets for Josh to meet could help him to carry out the plan successfully. **(4 marks)**

_____

_____

_____

_____

_____

_____

Ensuring safe environments in health and social care

Unit 4

This unit covers the following topics:

▶ potential hazards in health and social care environments

▶ the main principles of health and safety, and safeguarding legislation and guidelines for health and social care environments

▶ risk assessment processes related to health and social care.

Your learning in this unit will be assessed through assignments that are set and marked by your tutor in accordance with grading criteria and standards set by Edexcel. The assignments will require you to focus on:

▶ the range of hazards and risks to health, safety and security in health and social care environments

▶ applying knowledge and understanding of health and safety and safeguarding legislation and guidelines to a health and social care environment.

The questions and activities that follow provide you with an opportunity to develop your knowledge and assess your understanding of the range of topics that are part of Unit 4.

Answers can be found at: www.collinseducation.com/btechsc

4.1 Hazards and risks

Health and safety and safeguarding issues arise in all health and social care environments. The key to understanding health and safety and safeguarding issues is to think 'who is at risk?' and to identify aspects of the care environment (including behaviours) that can be hazardous to vulnerable people. The questions and activities that follow provide you with opportunities to develop and show your understanding of:

▶ *hazards*: as relevant to health and social care environments (e.g. rooms or outside recreational areas that pose a particular risk to individual service users); equipment/toys in a poor state of repair; incorrect storage of chemicals; inadequate control of infectious diseases; fire; poor working conditions; unsafe furnishings; inappropriate furnishings for patients/service users; inappropriate use of specialist equipment; insufficient equipment maintenance; poor staff training; lack of security measures; poor building maintenance; inadequate personal safety precautions; close proximity to radio transmissions; pollution of air and/or water; abuse

▶ *responsibilities*: employers, employees, service users.

Questions and activities

Tythebourne House is a private care home that is owned and run by Mary and Robert Pritchard. The Pritchards opened the home 3 years ago, and it offers care to older people. There are 16 residents living at the home. Mary has been checking for hazards that could be a health and safety risk to both residents and staff. She has checked the communal lounge and the residents' bedrooms. The lounge has antique rugs because Robert thinks it makes the room seem more welcoming. The lighting is kept subdued so that the residents can rest easily.

1. Checking for hazards in a care environment is a responsibility of care managers like Mary. Explain what is meant by the word 'hazard'. **(2 marks)**

_____

_____

2. The lounge at Tythebourne House is intended to be a welcoming and relaxing area. Identify two hazards for elderly residents in the lounge area. Explain why these hazards are a potential risk to the residents' health and safety. **(6 marks)**

_____

_____

_____

_____

_____

_____

3. Mary has checked for hazards in some of the areas of the home. List two other areas where it is important to check for hazards. **(2 marks)**

Area 1 _____

Area 2 _____

Sasha is one of the care workers at Tythebourne House. She has been asked to help one of the residents, Mr Smithson, to get out of bed and to bathe. Though she has not been trained to use the equipment, Sasha notices that the hoist that she needs to use has been broken and that Robert has made repairs to it himself. She also notices that the brakes don't work properly on Mr Smithson's bed.

4. Sasha knows that having working brakes on an elderly resident's bed is important for their health and safety. Describe two other possible hazards that could present a risk when she is working with Mr Smithson. **(4 marks)**

Hazard 1 _____

_____

Hazard 2 _____

_____

5. Explain what Sasha has a responsibility to do when she discovers the problem with the brakes on Mr Smithson's bed. **(2 marks)**

_____

_____

6. Whose responsibility is it to make sure that the environment is free of the sort of hazards that are present when Sasha is helping Mr Smithson? **(1 mark)**

_____

The Tulip Gardens Nursery caters for infants of 2 to 4 years of age. The nursery is located in a large housing estate and occupies the ground floor of a terraced house. Nasreen has begun working there as a nursery assistant. Karen owns and manages the nursery. She has shown Nasreen the facilities and equipment that the nursery provides. There is a main room containing a wide range of toys, books and play equipment that are spread out across the floor. A large climbing frame is in the centre of the room and space is very tight. The nursery keeps two pet guinea pigs. Karen explains that their cage has been moved to a corner of the kitchen area so that the children have more space to play.

7. Nasreen is worried that the main room of the nursery may have some hazards to health and safety. Can you give two reasons why she may have thought this? **(2 marks)**

   Reason 1 _____

   Reason 2 _____

8. Identify one other aspect of the nursery that could be a risk to health and safety. Explain why you think this may be a hazard. **(3 marks)**

   _____

   _____

   _____

   _____

Karen tells Nasreen that the nursery aims to provide a friendly, open environment and that the front door is left unlocked so that visitors can drop in.

9. Give two ways in which leaving the nursery's front door unlocked could be a risk to health and safety. **(2 marks)**

   Risk 1 _____

   _____

   Risk 2 _____

   _____

10. As the owner of the nursery, Karen has to fulfil her health and safety responsibilities. Which responsibility is she failing to fulfil by having an unlocked front door? **(1 mark)**

   _____

4.2 Health and safety legislation

A number of different laws have been passed to establish and enforce good standards of health and safety in care environments. The law on health and safety is regularly updated through the publication of new guidelines that care practitioners should know about and enforce. There is now an increased concern with safeguarding or protecting people who use care services from neglect and abuse when they are in receipt of care services. As a result, laws and regulations on the safeguarding of vulnerable adults are now also a part of the legal framework that care practitioners need to understand.

The questions and activities that follow provide you with opportunities to develop and show your understanding of:

▶ *relevant sections from appropriate legislation*: e.g. Health and Safety at Work Act; Food Safety Act; Food Safety (General Food Hygiene) Regulations; Manual Handling Operations Regulations; Reporting of Injuries, Diseases and Dangerous Occurrences Regulations (RIDDOR); Management of Health and Safety at Work Regulations; Control of Substances Hazardous to Health (COSHH) Regulations.

Questions and activities

Joe Ratcliff is the new deputy manager at the Fieldview Day Centre, a day care centre for older people. One of his responsibilities is as Health and Safety Officer for the centre. Joe has spent some time finding out about the health and safety legislation because he will need to ensure that the day centre is fulfilling its legal responsibilities. He knows about the Health and Safety at Work Act 1974, but he needs to find out more about other laws that aim to improve health and safety.

1. What is the name of the body, set up by the Health and Safety at Work Act 1974, that monitors standards and enforces health and safety law in the workplace in England? **(1 mark)**

_____

2. Can you list four of the legal responsibilities that the Fieldview Day Centre will need to meet under the Health and Safety at Work Act 1974? **(4 marks)**

Responsibility 1 _____

_____

Responsibility 2 _____

_____

Responsibility 3 _____

_____

Responsibility 4 _____

_____

Joe is worried that the Fieldview Day Centre may not be fulfilling its responsibilities under the Control of Substances Hazardous to Health (COSHH) Regulations 2002. He tells the centre manager that the centre does not seem to have a COSHH file, which it is required to have under the Regulations.

3. The centre manager asks Joe to explain what a COSHH file is and to describe what it should contain details of. What answer should Joe give? **(6 marks)**

_____

_____

_____

_____

_____

_____

_____

_____

4. Joe has inspected the kitchen at the Fieldview Day Centre where lunch and snacks for the clients are prepared. Can you name one piece of legislation that is aimed at ensuring good food hygiene? **(1 mark)**

5. One of the care workers at the Fieldview Day Centre is off work after injuring her back. It happened as she was helping a disabled client into his wheelchair. What is the name of the regulations that cover manual handling activities in the workplace? **(1 mark)**

4.3 Risk assessment processes

People who work in health and social care settings need to be aware of risk assessment processes. These identify, estimate and then try to minimise risks from the hazards that are present in health and social care settings. The questions and activities that follow provide you with opportunities to develop and show your understanding of:

▶ *identifying risks*: identifying hazards that could cause risks in everyday activities

▶ *estimating risk*: scale of risk; concept of likelihood of risk; degree of possible harm for different service user groups

▶ *controlling risks*: possible actions to reduce or remove risks

▶ *monitoring effectiveness of controls*: instructions for controlling risks; implementing controls; regular review of risks and controls; record keeping; roles of health and safety officer and care workers; policies and procedures

▶ *risks associated with everyday activities*: e.g. personal care; food preparation and eating; mobility and travel; work or education; hobbies/leisure.

Questions and activities

Joe decides to carry out a risk assessment at the Fieldview Day Centre. He wants to identify potential risks to the health, safety and security of the centre's clients, staff and visitors. Joe is inspecting the lounge, kitchen and other spaces in the day centre's building to look for environmental hazards that might be present. He is also looking at the centre's equipment and at the working practices of the centre staff.

1. Can you name an Act of Parliament or a regulation that requires employers to carry out a risk assessment in the workplace? **(1 mark)**

2. The Health and Safety Executive has identified five stages of a risk assessment. Can you list these five stages? **(5 marks)**

Stage 1 _____

_____

Stage 2 _____

_____

Stage 3 _____

_____

Stage 4 _____

_____

Stage 5 _____

_____

Joe has noticed that cleaning staff usually begin their work by collecting together and bagging up soiled and dirty linen. They then use the bag to prop open a fire door between the kitchen and the main lounge. The cleaners say that they do this because they find it quicker to plug a vacuum cleaner into a socket in the kitchen and run the lead through into the lounge. That way they can vacuum both rooms without unplugging the lead.

3. Describe three risks to health and safety that the cleaners are creating by working in this way. **(6 marks)**

Risk 1 _____

_____

Risk 2 _____

_____

Risk 3 _____

_____

4. As Health and Safety Officer for the day centre, what actions could Joe take to help the cleaning staff to work safely in the future? **(4 mark)**

_____

_____

_____

_____

_____

_____

5. Joe wants all the centre's staff to understand that they have a responsibility
   to help create a safe environment for staff and clients. One responsibility they
   have is to work safely. Describe two other responsibilities that employees
   have which are aimed at improving health and safety. **(4 marks)**

Responsibility 1 _____

_____

Responsibility 2 _____

_____

Cultural diversity in health and social care

This unit covers the following topics:

▶ the diversity of individuals in society

▶ beliefs and practices in different religious and secular groups

▶ factors that influence equality of opportunity

▶ legislation, codes of practice and charters that promote diversity.

Your learning in this unit will be assessed through assignments that are set and marked by your tutor in accordance with grading criteria and standards set by Edexcel. The assignments will require you to focus on:

▶ the diversity of individuals in society and the beliefs and practices in different religions or secular groups

▶ the factors that influence equality of opportunity for individuals and how legislation, codes of practice and charters promote diversity.

The questions and activities that follow provide you with an opportunity to develop your knowledge and assess your understanding of the range of topics that are part of Unit 6.

Answers can be found at: www.collinseducation.com/btechsc

6.1 The diversity of individuals and different religious beliefs and practices

We live in a society that is culturally diverse. Individuals differ in terms of their backgrounds and lifestyles, for example. These differences can have a big effect on individual needs and on how they are met. The questions and activities that follow provide you with opportunities to develop and show your understanding of:

▶ *social, cultural and political diversity*: relating to individuals in society (e.g. ethnicity, religious beliefs, secular beliefs, social class, gender, sexuality, age, family structure, disabilities).

Questions and activities

Jade is a district nurse in an inner city area. Jade works with a wide range of people and she needs to understand the differences between the many individuals that she cares for. Parveen is one of Jade's patients. She is 79 years old and moved to the UK from Pakistan 30 years ago.

Parveen lives with her husband, her daughter and her family, and her brother-in-law. Another of Jade's patients is Brian. Brian is 23 years old and lives alone. He was born in the local hospital and his family have lived in the area for several generations.

1. Jade says that she works in an area where there is a lot of diversity in the population. Can you explain what she means by this? **(2 marks)**

   _____

   _____

2. Parveen is of Asian extraction, whereas Brian describes his ethnicity as 'white British'. Can you describe three other ways in which Parveen is different from Brian? **(3 marks)**

   Difference 1 _____

   _____

   Difference 2 _____

   _____

   Difference 3 _____

   _____

3. Individuals are sometimes treated differently and unfairly because of their ethnicity. What is the term used for this sort of treatment? **(1 mark)**

   _____

4. Brian is planning to move in with his girlfriend, who has two children from a previous relationship. What type of family will Brian be living in after he moves? **(1 mark)**

   _____

5. Explain two reasons why it is important for Jade to take account of the differences between Parveen and Brian when she is working with them. **(4 marks)**

Reason 1 _____

_____

Reason 2 _____

_____

6.2 Beliefs and practices of different religious or secular groups

The United Kingdom is a religiously diverse country. The population of the UK includes members of a broad range of religious faith communities, though a significant section of the population also have no religious faith. The questions and activities that follow provide you with opportunities to develop and show your understanding of:

▶ *the range of religious/secular groups*: e.g. Christians, Hindus, atheists, Buddhists, humanists, Jehovah's Witnesses, Jews, Muslims, pagans, Rastafarians, Sikhs

▶ *beliefs and practices*: relating to different religious or secular groups (e.g. festivals and holy days, food, dress, symbols, forms of worship, health/medical beliefs).

Questions and activities

Peter is 47 years old and he describes himself as a Christian. He takes his faith seriously and follows the beliefs and practices of his religion. Davinda is also a devout believer. He is a Muslim and follows the beliefs and practices of his own faith.

1. Muslims and Christians are two of the faith groups that exist in UK society. There are also people in the UK who would see themselves as members of secular groups. Can you explain what is meant by the term 'secular group' and give one example? **(3 marks)**

_____

_____

_____

2. Apart from Muslims and Christians, can you name four other religious groups in UK society? **(4 marks)**

Religion 1 _____

Religion 2 _____

Religion 3 _____

Religion 4 _____

3. Members of different religious groups celebrate different festivals and holy days. Can you give two other ways in which the beliefs and practices of religious groups are different? **(2 marks)**

Difference 1 _____

Difference 2 _____

Steve is a physiotherapy assistant at the Deaconfield Health Centre. He deals with clients that belong to different groups and who use the services of the health centre. Steve has a good awareness of the beliefs and practices of the different religious and faith groups that clients of the health centre belong to.

4. Can you describe three factors that Steve would need to take into account when he deals with clients who are followers of the Islamic faith? **(6 marks)**

Factor 1 _____

_____

Factor 2 _____

_____

Factor 3 _____

_____

5. Give two reasons why Steve needs to have a good knowledge of the beliefs and practices of his clients. **(4 marks)**

Reason 1 _____

_____

Reason 2 _____

_____

6.3 Factors that influence equality of opportunity

There are a number of factors that can influence the opportunities available to different individuals in society. Equality of opportunity is important for everyone who uses, or may need to use, health and social care services. Challenging discrimination and using a non-discriminatory approach to care practice has an important influence on equality of opportunity. The questions and activities that follow provide you with opportunities to develop and show your understanding of:

▶ *social, cultural and political factors*: influences of, for example, ethnicity, religious beliefs, social class, gender, sexuality, age, family structure, disabilities

▶ *discriminatory practice*: prejudice, discrimination, stereotyping, labelling

- the effects of discrimination on an individual's health/wellbeing: physical, intellectual, emotional, social
- *non-discriminatory practice*: influences of, for example, individual worker responsibilities, institutional responsibilities, working with colleagues, working with users of services
- *materials*: equipment; activities; visual displays; toys and books that provide positive images of gender and race; avoidance of stereotyping
- *the role of the media*: books; leaflets, newspapers, magazines, television, internet.

Questions and activities

Melissa has been interviewed for post as a radiography assistant at The Aftonbury Clinic, a privately run health facility. She notices that all the other candidates, and the members of the interview panel, are male. As she is leaving Melissa overhears members of the interview panel discussing the applicants. One of the panel members says that he is glad they agreed not to appoint a female to the post. He says, 'Women are unreliable, they always get pregnant and leave their job'.

1. Melissa feels that she has been discriminated against. What is the name given to the type of discrimination that Melissa has suffered? **(1 mark)**

_____

_____

2. Melissa also feels that the comments of the panel members are stereotyping women. Can you explain what is meant by the term 'stereotyping'? **(2 marks)**

_____

_____

_____

_____

Rebecca is a new nursery assistant at the Playbright Nursery, which caters for up to 30 children from ages 1 to 4 years old. She is quite surprised to notice that there is only one black child attending the nursery, even though it is located in a multicultural housing estate where families from a range of ethnic and cultural backgrounds live. The nursery provides lunch and snacks for the children. The food, usually including ham for sandwiches, is bought from the local supermarket. Rebecca also notices that the toys and books in the nursery feature white, British children and that the displays and posters focus on Easter, Christmas and other Christian festivals. The nursery manager, Sharon, says that the nursery is open to all and that they welcome children from all races and backgrounds.

3. Can you explain why black families may be reluctant to send their children to the Playbright Nursery? **(3 marks)**

_____

_____

_____

4. Can you describe one thing the nursery is doing that indirectly discriminates against Jews, Muslims and members of some other religious groups? **(3 marks)**

_____

_____

_____

5. On her college course Rebecca learnt about the importance of non-discriminatory practice in care work. Can you explain what is meant by the term 'non-discriminatory practice'? **(2 marks)**

_____

_____

6. Can you describe two things that could be improved in the environment and facilities of the nursery that would support non-discriminatory practice? **(4 marks)**

Improvement 1 _____

_____

Improvement 2 _____

_____

6.4 Legislation, codes of practice and charters

Legislation, codes of practice and charters set out the rules or legal framework within which health and social care workers have to practice. This legal framework plays an important part in promoting equality and diversity. The questions and activities that follow provide you with opportunities to develop and show your understanding of:

▶ *role and impact of the following conventions, legislation and regulations (relevant sections)*: relevant and current sections of, for example, European Convention on Human Rights and Fundamental Freedoms; Mental Health Act; The Convention on the Rights of the Child; The Children Act; Race Relations (Amendment) Act; Disability Discrimination Act; Human Rights Act; Data Protection Act; Nursing and Residential Care Homes Regulations

▶ *codes of practice and charters*: relevant and current sections of, for example, General Social Care Council/Care Council for Wales/Northern Ireland Social Care Council codes of practice for social care workers and employers; charters; organisational policies; procedures and codes of practice

▶ *responsibilities*: employers, employees.

Questions and activities

Claire is 3 years old and is an only child. Claire lives with her mother, Tracy, and Tracy's partner Des, who moved in 6 months ago. Des often loses his temper with Claire and sometimes hits her severely. He also makes her go without food when he thinks she has been 'naughty'. Laura is a care assistant at the nursery that Claire attends. Laura has noticed the change in Claire over the past few months. She now seems underweight and is sometimes badly bruised.

1. What is the Act of Parliament that aims to protect vulnerable children like Claire? **(1 mark)**

_____

2. What action could Laura take to help prevent Claire from suffering further abuse? **(2 marks)**

_____

_____

Dennis is 28 years old and has had a successful career as an accountant. Dennis became disabled after a car accident 2 years ago and is now a wheelchair user. He was keen to resume his career after leaving hospital, but the firm he works for has offices in an old building that has two steps up to the front door. Dennis's boss says that if he can't get up to the office any longer he should find a new job.

3. Can you name the legislation that protects Dennis from discrimination on the basis of his disability? **(1 mark)**

_____

4. Can you describe one thing that Dennis's employer could do to support Dennis and to meet the firm's legal responsibilities? **(2 marks)**

_____

_____

_____

Glossary

Acute illness: short-term illness that occurs suddenly and may end quickly

Ageing process: the physical changes associated with growing older

Balanced diet: a diet that includes adequate amounts of all the nutrients needed for growth and activity

Care values: a range of core values or principles that guide the work of care practitioners

Cholesterol: a fat-like substance that is made by the body and carried in the blood; it also occurs in meat, dairy products and shellfish

Code of practice: a document that sets out standards for practice

Confidentiality: protecting the privacy of information, personal or otherwise, so that it is known only to those authorised to access it

Deprivation: lack of or absence of something

Dialect: a different form of a language (often affecting pronunciation) spoken in a particular area

Economic: related to money

Emotional: related to feelings

Empathy: the ability to understand or have compassion for the way another person may be feeling

Evaluate: make a judgement about something; assess a situation

Excrete: eliminate from the body

Gender: the term used for the biological, psychological and social differences between men and women

Holistic assessment: an evaluation or appraisal that relates to the 'whole' person and covers his or her physical, intellectual, emotional and social (PIES) needs

Immigration: the movement of people from one country into another country

Income: the amount of money people receive for working, from welfare benefits or other sources

Informal communication: familiar rather than formal ways of communicating, for example, casual or relaxed conversations, handwritten notes or text messages

Karma: the belief that one's actions in this life will determine one's destiny when one is reincarnated (reborn) in the next life

Labelling: defining or describing someone in a particular way, for example, by using an opinionated or judgemental word such as 'the depressed' or 'obsessive' person

Noxious: unpleasant; harmful or poisonous

Obesity: a condition characterised by excess body fat and a body mass index (BMI) of 30 or more

Paramount: supreme or major (often used when referring to 'importance')

Puberty: the period of physical growth that occurs during adolescence, when the body matures and is able to reproduce

Social class: a group of people who are similar in terms of income and status

Social diversity: when a population is socially mixed and includes people from many different backgrounds

Stereotyping: talking or thinking about an individual or group of people in a simplified and often negative way, for example, 'all young women are ...'

Surgical interventions: performing operations; surgery

Unfair discrimination: treating someone differently or unjustly

Verbal communication: communicating using words, for example, conversation

Welfare state: the term used to describe a state in which the government plays a key role in providing health, social care and education services

Student notes